Cheltenham racecourse
PITVILLE PUMP ROOM
PRESTBURY
Pitville Park
Evesham Road
Pitville Lawn
Albert Road
Prestbury Road
Cromwell Road
Clyde Crescent
Priors Road
Cheltenham Town FC
Whaddon Road
WHADDON
Pittville Circus Road
All Saints Road
Hewlett Road
Harp Hill
w Road
Hales Road
Berkeley Street
Hewlett Road
Carlton Street
Stanley Road
Battledown Approach
dford Park
Coltham Fields
Kevnisham Road
London Road
Old Bath Road
Charlton Park
CHARLTON KINGS
Cirencester Road
London Road
Cudnall Street
AF470570
Key
Train station
Bus station
School
Church
Fire station
Information

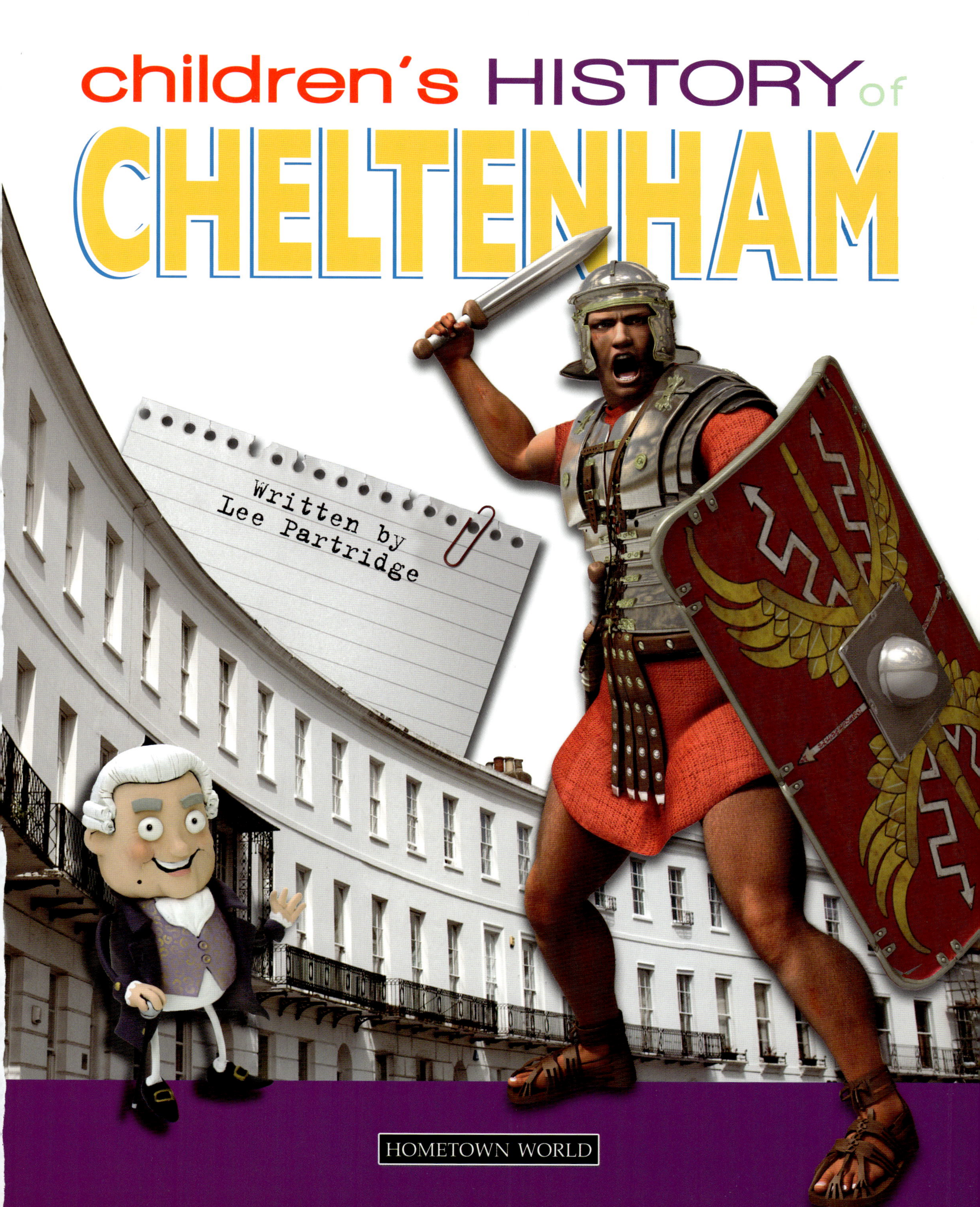

children's HISTORY of
CHELTENHAM
Written by Lee Partridge
HOMETOWN WORLD

How well do you know your town?

Have you ever wondered what it would have been like living in Cheltenham when the Romans arrived? What about fighting in the Civil War? This book will uncover the important and exciting things that happened in your town.

Want to hear the other good bits? You will love this book! Some rather brainy folk have worked on it to make sure it's fun and informative. So what are you waiting for? Peel back the pages and be amazed at what happened in your town.

Timeline shows which period (dates and people) each spread is talking about

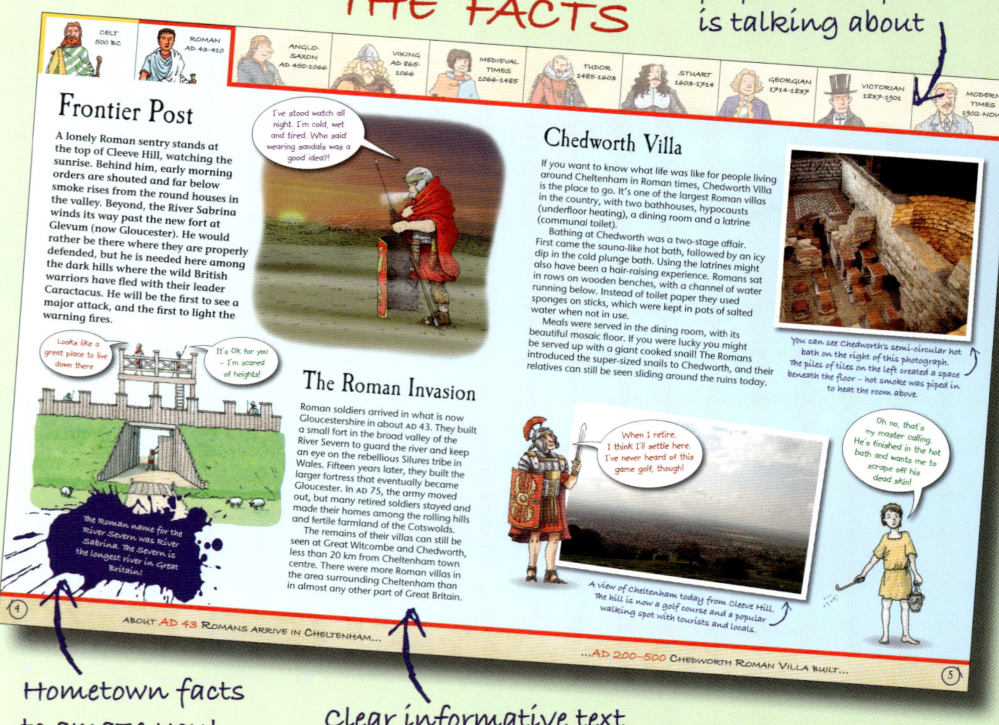

Hometown facts to amaze you!

Clear informative text

THE EVIDENCE

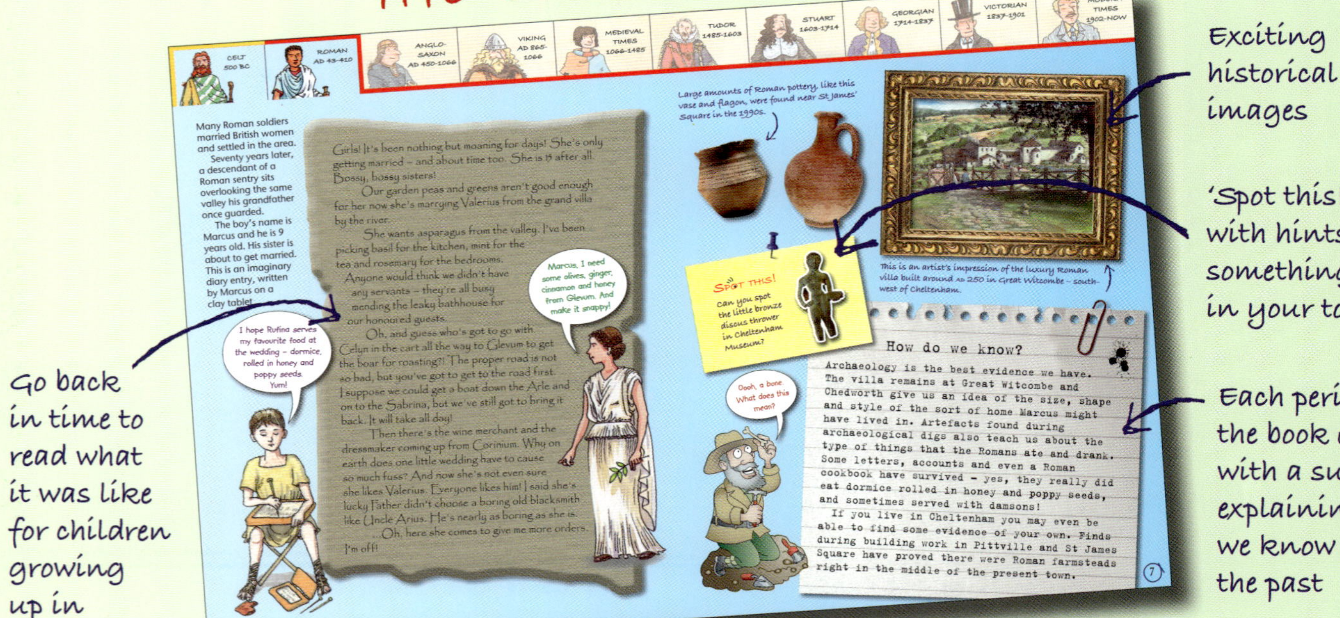

Go back in time to read what it was like for children growing up in Cheltenham

Exciting historical images

'Spot this!' game with hints on something to find in your town

Each period in the book ends with a summary explaining how we know about the past

VIKING
MEDIEVAL TIMES
TUDOR
STUART
GEORGIAN
VICTORIAN
MODERN TIMES
AD 800
AD 900
1000
1100
1200
1300
1400
1500
1600
1700
1800
1900
2000

Contents

Frontier Post

A lonely Roman sentry stands at the top of Cleeve Hill, watching the sunrise. Behind him, early morning orders are shouted and far below smoke rises from the round houses in the valley. Beyond, the River Sabrina winds its way past the new fort at Glevum (now Gloucester). He would rather be there where they are properly defended, but he is needed here among the dark hills where the wild British warriors have fled with their leader Caractacus. He will be the first to see a major attack, and the first to light the warning fires.

The Roman name for the River Severn was River Sabrina. The Severn is the longest river in Great Britain!

The Roman Invasion

Roman soldiers arrived in what is now Gloucestershire in about AD 43. They built a small fort in the broad valley of the River Severn to guard the river and keep an eye on the rebellious Silures tribe in Wales. Fifteen years later, they built the larger fortress that eventually became Gloucester. In AD 75, the army moved out, but many retired soldiers stayed and made their homes among the rolling hills and fertile farmland of the Cotswolds.

The remains of their villas can still be seen at Great Witcombe and Chedworth, less than 20 km from Cheltenham town centre. There were more Roman villas in the area surrounding Cheltenham than in almost any other part of Great Britain.

Chedworth Villa

If you want to know what life was like for people living around Cheltenham in Roman times, Chedworth Villa is the place to go. It's one of the largest Roman villas in the country, with two bathhouses, hypocausts (underfloor heating), a dining room and a latrine (communal toilet).

Bathing at Chedworth was a two-stage affair. First came the sauna-like hot bath, followed by an icy dip in the cold plunge bath. Using the latrines might also have been a hair-raising experience. Romans sat in rows on wooden benches, with a channel of water running below. Instead of toilet paper they used sponges on sticks, which were kept in pots of salted water when not in use.

Meals were served in the dining room, with its beautiful mosaic floor. If you were lucky you might be served up with a giant cooked snail! The Romans introduced the super-sized snails to Chedworth, and their relatives can still be seen sliding around the ruins today.

You can see Chedworth's semi-circular hot bath on the right of this photograph. The piles of tiles on the left created a space beneath the floor – hot smoke was piped in to heat the room above.

A view of Cheltenham today from Cleeve Hill. The hill is now a golf course and a popular walking spot with tourists and locals.

Many Roman soldiers married British women and settled in the area.

Seventy years later, a descendant of a Roman sentry sits overlooking the same valley his grandfather once guarded.

The boy's name is Marcus and he is 9 years old. His sister is about to get married. This is an imaginary diary entry, written by Marcus on a clay tablet...

Girls! It's been nothing but moaning for days! She's only getting married – and about time too. She is 15 after all. Bossy, bossy sisters!

Our garden peas and greens aren't good enough for her now she's marrying Valerius from the grand villa by the river.

She wants asparagus from the valley. I've been picking basil for the kitchen, mint for the tea and rosemary for the bedrooms.

Anyone would think we didn't have any servants – they're all busy mending the leaky bathhouse for our honoured guests.

Oh, and guess who's got to go with Celyn in the cart all the way to Glevum to get the boar for roasting?! The proper road is not so bad, but you've got to get to the road first. I suppose we could get a boat down the Arle and on to the Sabrina, but we've still got to bring it back. It will take all day!

Then there's the wine merchant and the dressmaker coming up from Corinium. Why on earth does one little wedding have to cause so much fuss? And now she's not even sure she likes Valerius. Everyone likes him! I said she's lucky Father didn't choose a boring old blacksmith like Uncle Arius. He's nearly as boring as she is.

...Oh, here she comes to give me more orders. I'm off!

Large amounts of Roman pottery, like this vase and flagon, were found near St James Square in the 1990s.

This is an artist's impression of the luxury Roman villa built around AD 250 in Great Witcombe – south-west of Cheltenham.

SPOT THIS!

Can you spot the little bronze discus thrower in Cheltenham Museum?

How do we know?

Archaeology is the best evidence we have. The villa remains at Great Witcombe and Chedworth give us an idea of the size, shape and style of the sort of home Marcus might have lived in. Artefacts found during archaeological digs also teach us about the type of things that the Romans ate and drank. Some letters, accounts and even a Roman cookbook have survived – yes, they really did eat dormice rolled in honey and poppy seeds, and sometimes served with damsons!

If you live in Cheltenham you may even be able to find some evidence of your own. Finds during building work in Pittville and St James Square have proved there were Roman farmsteads right in the middle of the present town.

Kingdom of the Hwicce

Twin brothers Eanhere and Eanfrith thunder into the Severn Vale on horseback with their servants following close behind. Their kingdom lies before them: farmsteads, mills, sheep, the great river and the great roads. The ground is iron hard from frost. They will welcome a warming cup of mead from the British holy men at the monastery nearby.

The Saxons came to Britain from north-western Europe in about AD 450 as farmers and traders, but they also fought for land.

Prime Location

In Saxon times, England as we know it didn't exist. It was divided into small kingdoms with different rulers. The area where Cheltenham now stands was part of the Hwicce kingdom, close to its capital of Winchcombe.

Eanhere and Eanfrith are thought to have been the first kings of Hwicce. With the River Severn and Roman roads linking the area to the rest of the country, they were in a good position as many people would have passed through their kingdom on their travels around the country.

Celtenhomme

The Anglo-Saxon settlement of Celtenhomme began where the Roman road from Winchcombe to Gloucester ran close to a stream – the River Chelt. Celtenhomme, meaning 'village under the hill', can be thought of as the true beginning of the town of Cheltenham. It was the site of a monastery from AD 790, providing local people with work as carpenters, smiths and farmers. The royal palace at nearby Winchcombe would have made the villagers feel safe.

Spot this!

See if you can spot this brooch in Cheltenham Museum. It was found next to a skeleton's shoulder in an Anglo-Saxon grave near Bishop's Cleeve.

How do we know?

We know a lot about Saxon Cheltenham from the Domesday Book, completed in 1086. The book was created for William the Conquerer, and listed all the land owners in the country in Saxon times. It also listed all the places conquered by the Normans, including two mills in Cheltenham.

In May 2010, archaeologists made an important discovery on the building site of a new school near Cheltenham town centre. They unearthed a large Anglo-Saxon feasting hall, fragments of pottery and two skeletons. This is exciting new evidence of Cheltenham as an important Anglo-Saxon settlement.

We know about the Priory that stood near Cheltenham's present-day High Street from AD 790 because there are records of arguments between the Bishops of Worcester and Hereford over who owned it.

Place names can survive for hundreds of years. Can you think of any places in and around Cheltenham that include the following Anglo-Saxon words?

Saxon	English
brock	badger
combe	deep valley
worth	enclosure
beck	small stream
ford	river crossing
dun	hill

Market Day

The long track of the village is packed with traders. Fresh celery and watercress lie next to rotting parsnips, onions and pears. The herb wife has her recipes and remedies. Pigs, geese, hens and goats grunt, squawk and bleat for attention. A child hopefully offers fresh primroses to a well-dressed lady. The ribbon seller spreads good news. Lady Matilda will be queen after all!

Empress Matilda

The Middle Ages started in 1066, when William the Conqueror took the English crown. His youngest son, Henry, became king in 1100. But when he died in 1135 there was only his daughter Matilda to succeed him. Some people didn't want to be ruled by a woman and chose her cousin Stephen instead.

The Duke of Gloucester was Matilda's half brother, and he was on her side. As was Milo, the constable of England and Gloucester castle. The people of Cheltenham would have been required to support their Duke and Empress Matilda.

...1135 Stephen seizes the throne from his cousin Matilda...

Uncertain Times

Gloucester was the centre of the rebellion against Stephen, so life in Cheltenham must have been uncertain and frightening. Food and property were often stolen from the locals by Milo's warriors and Stephen's soldiers.

In 1141, Stephen was taken prisoner which meant Matilda was finally free to rule. To thank Milo for his support, Matilda made him Earl of Hereford and gave him lands including Cheltenham. But she was only in power for a few months and was never crowned. Unrest continued for years, and more people took sides with Stephen. He ruled until his death in 1154 but it was Matilda's son, Henry II, who became king after him.

St Mary's Church has a ring of 12 bells, also known as a 'peal of bells'. Most churches have six or eight bells.

SPOT THIS!

St Mary's Church has a famous rose window – can you spot it? Visit on a sunny afternoon for a spectacular light show!

St Mary's Church

St Mary's Church in the town centre is Cheltenham's oldest building. It is believed to stand on the site of an Anglo-Saxon church, and was built in the late 1100s. It is the only medieval building left in Cheltenham. The church was first extended in the 13th century so that more people could attend. The north and south aisles were added, and the now leaning spire. The church has continued to change over the years. The beautiful stained glass windows were added in the 1800s.

This is an imaginary conversation between two girls, gossiping in Leckhampton. They are maids to the DeSpencer family, and should be busy collecting ribbons and thread from the carter who's just come back from market.

The name Leckhampton means 'homestead where leeks are grown'.

Shhh, Hawise. He'll hear you!

But it's so funny, Winifred. He thinks he's the finest knight in the land, even with a toy sword and mud all over his tunic.

Yes, but look what skill he has. I know he's only got a wooden sword, but he wields it well.

About as well as he wields a toothpick!

You are terrible! My lord has excellent table manners.

Well, he eats like a horse…but I bet he can't ride one! He's hardly going to gallop off on a white stallion and fight for England.

Shhh! If the rebels come, we may all have to fight.

But on who's side, Wini? The Court has been given to the 'king', but surely we should support my Lady and the Duke. Not that there's anything here to fight for – only churches, peasants and leeks!

How can you say such things Hawise, when battle could be upon us!

Oh, quick, straighten your headscarf – Mistress Edith is heading this way to check our spinning, and we haven't even got the thread yet!

A Land Fit for a King

In the 1200s, Cheltenham grew from a farming settlement into a small market town. It remained in royal hands until 1247, when Henry III swapped it for the towns of Winchelsea and Rye, owned by an order of French monks.

Cheltenham must have been valuable as the monks held on to the town for nearly 170 years. While they were in charge, the churches in Leckhampton and Charlton Kings were placed under the control of St Mary's in Cheltenham.

It took Henry V and an Act of Parliament in 1414 to get Cheltenham back in the ownership of English royalty.

How do we know?

The Domesday Book is an excellent source of information. We know that Leckhampton, recorded as Lechametone and Lechantone, was divided among three landowners.

The book also tells us that Cheltenham, recorded as Chinteneha, was the 'king's land' with a population in 1086 of 114 people.

Up Hatherley is referred to as 'the hawthorne clearing', and Swindon Village as 'the village where pigs are kept'.

Many official documents survive today carrying their sender's seal. The seals were made by a 'matrice', a metal stamp, and this was pressed into wax. A ribbon or tie attached the seal to the document. If the document was tampered with the seal would break.

These wax seals belonging to Matilda and Stephen were attached to official documents to confirm the sender and keep them private.

Leckhampton Court was built in the 1300s by John Giffard, who owned the Manor of Leckhampton after 1327. It was one of the grandest manor houses in medieval Gloucestershire. It now belongs to Sue Ryder Care and serves as a hospice for sick people.

Tudor Times

A ragged child swats at flies that buzz around her ears and crawl on her grubby bare feet. If she had the energy, she would follow the stray dogs to the River Chelt. It's shallow this time of year, and smelly, but it would be cooling. Around her the grown-ups blither on, "The queen is coming. No – not here, you fool – to Sudeley…" The ragged girl wonders if the queen wears a golden crown. Will they feast on pheasant? She can't quite remember the last time she ate.

Henry VIII's sixth, and last, wife Katherine Parr spent the last years of her life at Sudeley Castle in Winchcombe.

Catholic or Protestant?

Around 1530, Henry VIII fell out with the Catholic pope over his divorce from the queen, Catherine of Aragon. He declared himself head of the Church of England and decided to shut down all the religious houses and seize their land and valuable possessions. This was known as the 'Dissolution of the Monasteries'. St Mary's Church in Cheltenham became the property of the Crown.

Many Catholics in England were unhappy because they thought the pope should be head of the Church. Edward VI, Henry's son and heir, passed a law which made the country Protestant. Later his half sister, Mary, tried to make England Catholic again. Many people, rich and poor, died for their beliefs during this time. Those who disagreed with the king or queen were often burnt at the stake.

Spot this!

In 1782, Katherine Parr's coffin was discovered in the ruins of Sudeley Castle, where she died in 1548. A lock of hair, removed from her corpse, can still be seen there today.

Pate's Progress

Landowner and Member of Parliament Richard Pate was born in Cheltenham, and probably went to school in the parish church. He would have seen the effect the Dissolution had on poor families, who relied on the monasteries for education and other help. In 1574, Pate founded a grammar school in Cheltenham for 50 boys. He also built almshouses, where the poor could live and be looked after.

Pate's Grammar School still exists over 430 years later, but it has moved to new buildings. It is now open for girls as well as boys.

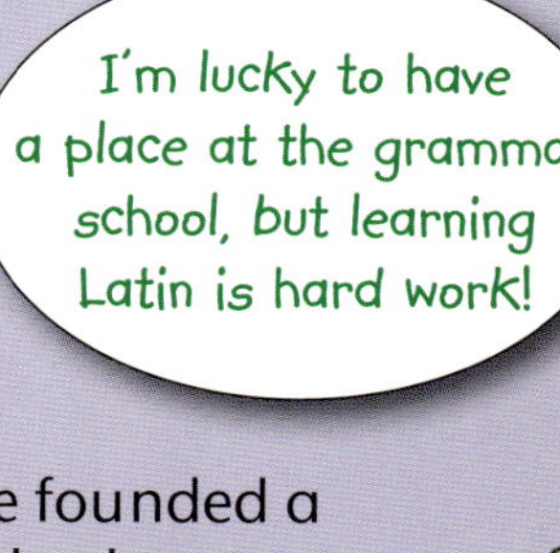

The Grammar School was originally situated by the brewery on the High Street. It later moved to Princess Elizabeth Way.

Tobacco Farming

Having lived at Sudeley Castle as a teenager, and visited there as an adult, Queen Elizabeth I would have known Cheltenham.

It was the queen's support for explorers such as Francis Drake and Walter Raleigh that brought exotic crops to the town. Walter Raleigh and Richard Pate may well have met at Elizabeth's court, and tobacco plants were first introduced to the parish in 1565. The crops flourished but, unfortunately for local farmers, growing tobacco became illegal in the 1600s.

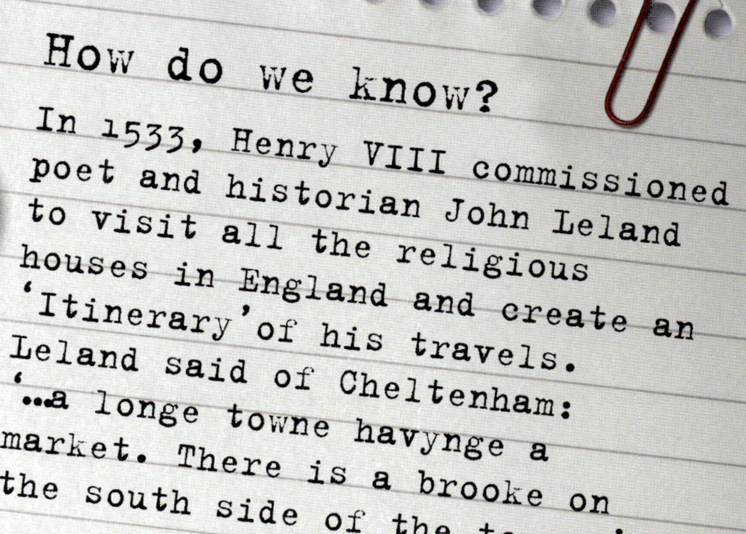

Civil War

Even at dusk the heat is stifling. Our battle weary King's Cavaliers sit and wait. For weeks we have besieged the city of Gloucester, but word has come that a massive Parliamentarian army approaches from the east. Are we expected to give up after all this time? Surely we can overcome those within the battered walls before the Earl of Essex arrives. We far outnumber them and their defence won't hold up against our army...or will it?

Charles I believed that he had been chosen by God to rule England.

King versus Country

In 1642, the English Civil War broke out. Many people did not like the way the king ruled or the way he treated people who criticized him. When the war started, families were split in two – with many fathers and sons fighting on opposite sides.

In 1643, King Charles I's army camped near Cheltenham. Charles demanded the surrender of Gloucester, but the people didn't give in and Charles besieged the city with an army of thousands. Inside, about 1,000 soldiers held the defence with the help of the townspeople. Parliamentary relief forces reached Cheltenham on 5th September, and the king retreated under the cover of night. He skirted around the Parliamentarians, taking refuge at Sudeley Castle on 7th September. The next day, the Earl of Essex led the relief troops into Gloucester in triumph.

The Battlefield

Because of its central position, Cheltenham was trampled over by one army after the other, each trying to gain control of towns in the area. Cleeve Hill provided a good viewpoint, and local manor houses became base camps. Thousands of soldiers needed food, shelter and weapons. The local people had to supply these whether they liked it or not. Food was scarce, and any surviving crops may well have lain in the field as many farmers were away fighting. Caught between two armies, Cheltenham would have been a desperate place to live during the Civil War years.

SPOT THIS!

These Charles I silver coins were found in Winchcombe. Can you spot them at Cheltenham Museum?

How do we know?

In the 1800s, Civil War relics were found in Jessop's Gardens and at Charlton Kings. Later, in 1997, a hoard of silver coins was found in Winchcombe, north of Sudeley Castle. It is thought that the coins, found along with fragments of a clay jug, were buried for safe-keeping in 1644, when the area was in the middle of the battles and bloodshed of the Civil War.

The Octagon Tower at Sudeley Castle still bears the marks of cannon balls fired when Parliamentarians attacked in 1644.

Sudeley Castle was a Royalist headquarters during the Civil War, but was left in ruins afterwards.

Royal Cheltenham Spa

It is as if all of Cheltenham has crowded into the High Street. Thankfully the road is repaired and the river no longer stagnates in the middle, trickling instead in channels either side. The excitement and heat beneath bonnets and wigs is intense. This is their last chance to glimpse King George III as his coach trundles past. The event brings the whole town together, well almost. To the south (the spa side) gather the genteel types. The less well off cluster to the north. "God save the King!" goes up the cry.

Pigeons and Pumps

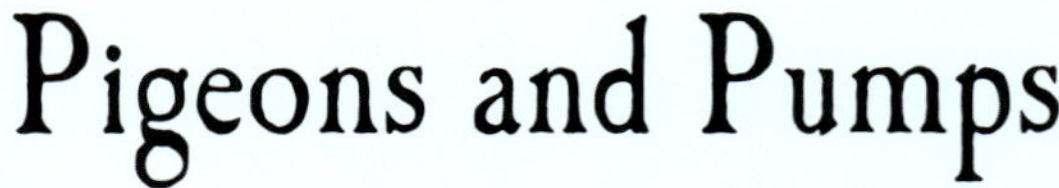

In 1716, locals discovered Cheltenham's first healing spring after seeing pigeons pecking at mineral deposits on the ground. William Mason owned the land at the time, where Cheltenham Ladies College is today. Mason quickly decided to bottle and sell the water, but it took 20 years before his daughter Elizabeth and her husband Henry Skillicorne truly developed the site.

In 1740, a certain Dr Short found the water "superior to any in the country". Tree-lined avenues and a pump room were added, attracting around 600 visitors a year. Eventually, the king himself arrived in 1788 and Cheltenham became the toast of fashionable society. Jane Austen, Lord Byron and the Duke of Wellington were some of the famous people who visited Cheltenham.

Entertainment

By 1824 – during the reign of George IV – over 17,000 people lived in Cheltenham. But much of the town you can see today was built for its visitors. They required ballrooms, theatres, grand houses and entertainment, such as the horse racing at Cleeve Hill. The first Cheltenham Gold Cup was held in 1819. But the people of Cheltenham began to believe that the gambling at the races was wicked, and in 1829 the grandstand was burned to the ground. Despite this, the event has survived and the racecourse now covers 200 hectares.

Health for All

The water attracted, and may have benefited, many wealthy visitors to Cheltenham. In turn the health of the town was improved by one of those visitors. Dr Edward Jenner brought his wife Katherine to take the waters. He was so impressed by their good effect that he returned every summer for 25 years. At this time, Jenner was developing the smallpox vaccine that would later save thousands of lives. In 1769, smallpox killed 12 per cent of the population of Cheltenham. It is known that Jenner gave his vaccine free of charge to the poor from his house in St Georges Place.

This cartoon shows Edward Jenner administering the smallpox vaccination. People are sprouting cows from their bodies – this didn't really happen!

SPOT THIS!

Jenner's house was knocked down in the 1970s, but a replica was built in 1994. Can you spot the blue plaque by the door?

Pitt's Pump Room

Completed in 1830, the Pump Room was the largest and last of the spa buildings built in Cheltenham. It was part of local landowner Joseph Pitt's plan to develop the area around the spa as 'Pittville'. The Greek temple design, grand ballroom and marble pump show how far Cheltenham had come in 50 years.

The Pump Room overlooks Pittville Park.

Unlike most spa towns, Cheltenham had a number of small spas – each with its own special healing properties. The water in each spa contained different minerals, and had its own unique flavour and smell.

This is a made-up letter from a 10-year-old boy called Charles. He is visiting Cheltenham with his father, and writing home to his mother in London.

Dearest Mother,

Father and I are having a wonderful summer in Cheltenham, and the ulcers on Father's legs are starting to heal already!

We are woken at 6 every morning, and we walk up to the Pump Room through the gardens. If I have a little bread left from breakfast, Father lets me feed it to the birds on the lake while he takes a rest.

Then we continue our walk. Father takes a whole glassful of the water each morning and another after supper. On the first day, he let me try it too. It was worse than Cook's soup – as salty as the sea, and with a whiff of bad eggs! Yuck! Father says, if it's good enough for the King then it's good enough for us, but I don't think I'll try it again all the same!

The rest of the day is ours. I have made a friend called Elinor. She's come to Pitville Spa with her older brother, William. He has the most horrific pimples, and I have to say that the waters have yet to have an effect!

I can't wait for you and little Henry to come and join us. Father has promised that we can go and watch the horse racing on Cleeve Hill, and then have tea at the hotel. I think you would love it here. There are fine ladies and beautiful gardens everywhere you look.

It's 8 o'clock now and I have to be up early again tomorrow, so goodnight Mother.

Your Loving Son,
Charles

PITTVILLE SPA
CHELTENHAM

A MOST IMPORTANT DISCOVERY…

FOR THE ABSOLUTE CURE OF: pimples, ulcers of the legs, female disorders and many other troublesome ailments.

The value of this water consists in it being so highly concentrated as to be capable of transport without inconvenience, at the same time that its medical qualities remain totally unaltered. The result of which is a clear and bright water, having six times the strength of the water obtained from the spring.

TAKE THE WATERS AT PITTVILLE SPA – A UNIQUE AND MOST AGREEABLE CURE!

SPOT THIS!

Montpellier Spa was opened in 1821 in a building known as the Rotunda. The building is still there today. Can you find it? Here's a clue: it's now a bank, not a spa!

How do we know?

By Georgian times, there were plenty of written records including diaries, government papers and newspapers to tell us what was happening in Cheltenham. Not everyone liked the town.

On 30th September 1826, the famous diarist William Cobbett had this to say: "Cheltenham, which is what they call a 'watering place'; that is to say, a place to which gluttons, drunkards...of all descriptions resort, in the hope of getting rid of the bodily consequences of their...sins. When I enter a place like this, I always feel disposed to squeeze up my nose with my fingers."

Cheltenham is home to more complete Georgian buildings than anywhere else in England. Walk around the town to get an idea of how it would have looked in Regency times. Look out for the different types of window, balcony and column.

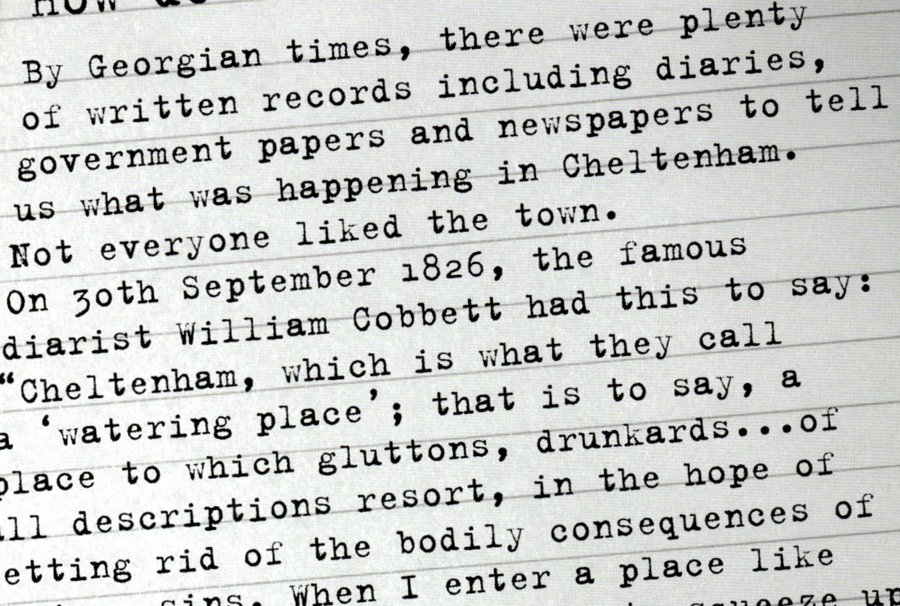

The sedan chair was a popular form of transport for wealthy people in Georgian times. A law was passed in Cheltenham preventing sedan chairs from being parked on the pavement when not in use.

During World War Two, Pitville Pump Room was used as a storage depot by the American and British armies.

Montpellier Walk

Busy, bustling, bonnets and boots jostle in the High Street – fast becoming the lower end of town. Turning the corner, caps and shawls give way to fine gloves and parasols as ladies and gentlemen take the warm spring air on the Promenade. Only a select few venture beyond to the elegant Montpellier Walk.

This is what the Montpellier Walk looked like around 1843. Can you spot the Rotunda, and St Mary's Church spire in the background?

In 1837, locals gathered excitedly in Montpellier Gardens to watch daring balloonist Charles Green take off in his Great Nassau Air Balloon.

Fit For a Queen

In 1837, Victoria was made queen, ruling over the vast and rich British Empire. Many people were proud of the Empire – likening it to those of Ancient Greece and Rome. The Queen's Hotel in Cheltenham was built in celebration in 1838, and it is still open over 170 years later. Under Queen Victoria, Cheltenham continued to develop. Trees in Montpellier Walk were removed to make way for an impressive row of shops designed by architect W. H. Knight. The rich and famous flocked to the now fashionable town. When writer Charles Dickens visited he said, "Rarely have I seen such a place that so attracted my fancy."

A pair of statues decorate the shop fronts on Montpellier Walk. The female figures are Ancient Greek in style, and take the form of columns, supporting the building above on their heads.

Developing World

Cheltenham benefited from developments in technology during Victorian times, even though it was not an industrial town. The railway linked Cheltenham to London and Birmingham in 1842, and to Bristol in 1844. In 1847, a second station opened in the town. In 1849, 5,000 children watched Queen Victoria's train pass by as she travelled to the Isle of Wight from Scotland.

The more fortunate people of Cheltenham also gained electric lights, telephones, better sewers and even motor cars.

The Queen's Hotel overlooks Imperial Gardens. Can you imagine what it would have been like here in Queen Victoria's time? What might you have seen in place of taxis and coffee shops?

Pupils in the Lower Hall at Cheltenham Ladies College. This photo was taken in about 1894. How do you think school life has changed since then?

Rich and Educated

Cheltenham attracted the wealthy, and in Victorian times three exclusive private schools opened in the town. Cheltenham Ladies College was founded in 1854, but it was when Dorothea Beale became principal in 1858 that the college began to establish its excellent reputation. Beale was a campaigner for women's rights, and was determined to provide a true academic education for girls. The college grew rapidly, soon needing larger promises and taking over the original spa buildings. It remains in the same location today, and is still considered one of the best private girls' schools in the country.

Helping the Poor

Although Cheltenham was thought of as a well-to-do town and a pleasant place to live, this wasn't true for everyone. Cheltenham Poor Law Union was formed in 1835 to help offer relief to those in need.

Cheltenham's workhouses provided food and shelter for adults and children with nowhere else to go. The people who lived there were called 'inmates'. In 1841, a new workhouse for 581 inmates and a girls' orphanage also opened their doors. Five years later, a home for unmarried mothers and a soup kitchen were opened. At Christmas in 1869, dinner was served in the Market Hall for 500 poor children and, 10 years later, bread and coal were given to 1,700 needy locals.

Agnes Hennesey is the name of one of the real inmates at the Cheltenham Workhouse. This is an imaginary diary extract by Agnes, aged 12, written on 7th November 1881 – the day she entered the workhouse with her mother, younger brother and sister.

Tuesday

When Father was alive, he worked on the railway. We wasn't rich, but we had enough to eat and shoes on our feet. But he died last winter from typhoid, and then my sister Ellen too. No one knew until it was too late that it was from drinking the dirty water from the well in the park.

Mother and I have tried so hard to keep the family together. But it aint no good. She can't make enough money dressmaking to feed us all. And my wages are hardly any help, even though I work 12 hours a day. The littl'uns are cold and hungry every night. We have no choice but to come here, even though it means we will be split up...

Famous Cheltonians

Cheltenham was the birthplace of some world-famous people who lived during Victorian times.

Edward Adrian Wilson was born in 1872 on Montpellier Terrace. He was a pupil at Cheltenham College, and later became a doctor and wildlife artist. Wilson joined Captain Robert Falcon Scott on his 1901 expedition to the Antarctic. Then, in 1912, Wilson accompanied Scott to the South Pole. Wilson died on the expedition along with Scott and three others. There is a memorial to him in the Long Gardens in the Promenade.

Gustav Holst was born in 1874 at 4 Pittville Terrace – now Clarence Road. His grandfather was a composer and taught the harp. His father was organist and choirmaster at All Saints Church in Pittville, and his mother was a singer. Gustav studied at Cheltenham Grammar School. He loved music and dedicated his life to it. His masterpiece, "The Planets", took two years to write and is still performed today.

The house in which Holst grew up is now a museum. You can see some of his belongings there, including the piano on which he composed "The Planets".

How do we know?

The Victorians left us a lot of evidence, such as photographs, archives, records and newspaper clippings. Looking at the 1881 census tells us a little about the inmates of the Cheltenham Workhouse.

Name	Married	Age	Sex	Relation	Occupation	Birthplace
Agnes HENNESEY	U	12	F	Pauper	Scholar	Cheltenham
Arthur HENNESEY	U	10	M	Pauper	Scholar	Cheltenham
Olive HENNESEY	U	7	F	Pauper	Scholar	Cheltenham
Ruth HENNESEY	W	33	F	Pauper	Dressmaker	Cheltenham

These children were here with their mother. Perhaps their father had died or left. She had a trade, but it seems she could not earn enough to feed all her children.

SP☉T THIS!

In 2008, a statue of Holst was placed in the centre of a fountain in Imperial Gardens. What is shown on the eight plaques around the base of the statue?

Wartime

There was a terrible air raid last week. It felt like the sky was raining bombs, and was the worst one so far. Only now does Mum think it's safe to queue for food again. We've been making do with what we've grown in the garden, but we're desperate for some meat. A meat and potato pie, sounds like heaven! Our ration books have become one of our most prized possessions. I know Mum keeps hers next to the bed when she goes to sleep – for fear of losing it!

This photo, taken in about 1944, shows people queuing for potatoes at Collyers Markets Ltd in the Colonnade. The queue stretched all the way to the Promenade.

Wartime Life

Even though Cheltenham managed to escape much damage during the World War Two, people still had to change the way they lived. They carried gas masks in case gas bombs were dropped, and when the sirens went, they had to run to air-raid shelters.

The Germans had cut off supplies from abroad, so food became scarce. People were given ration books, which meant they were only allowed a small amount of things like meat, eggs, sugar and cheese. This way, everyone had a fair share. Rationing of some foods didn't end until 1954, and the last thing to go was meat.

Many allies, including the American Forces, were stationed in Cheltenham. The Pittville Pump Room was used as a base for the Americans during the war and some schools were also taken over.

...1940 155 bombs dropped on Cheltenham...

Bombings and Defence

Air-raid shelters were built and iron railings were removed to make weapons. Thousands of evacuees arrived from Birmingham and London, but even Cheltenham was bombed. On the night of 11th December, 1940, 155 bombs were dropped and 23 people killed. Hitler had decided to attack all the 'beautiful' cities in the hope of breaking people's spirits. German prisoners of war were billeted in Leckhampton. Some remained after the war and married local girls.

Gas masks were made for animals such as dogs and cats.

Bomb damage on Brunswick Street.

GCHQ

After the war the Government Communications Headquarters were moved from London. Cheltenham was chosen as the new location because of its excellent transport links with all parts of the country. The move happened in 1951 and GCHQ still operates, providing intelligence to the armed forces.

How do we know?

We know that people used gas masks during wartime to protect themselves. Many gas masks can be seen in museums, in surprisingly good condition as they were actually rarely needed. There are also written accounts of people who lived during the war, and of course the stories of people still living who experienced the events first hand.

Some air-raid shelters still remain and a few houses in Rodborough Avenue even have them at the bottom of their gardens!

Cheltenham Today and Tomorrow...

We know about the history of Cheltenham from what people have left behind. Written records, archaeological digs and buildings are just some of the things that help tell us about the past. But what will we leave behind to tell our children and our children's children?

The Wishing Fish Clock was designed in 1985. It is 14 metres tall and can be seen in the Regent Arcade. Will it still be there in a 100 years' time?

Cheltenham College has been a school since 1841. How will schooling change in the next 100 years?

Every half an hour the fish blows bubbles from the Wishing Fish Clock. If you catch a bubble you can make a wish.

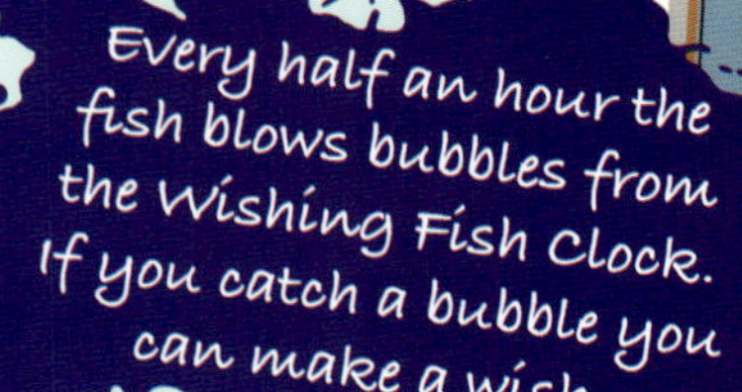

Cheltenham Racecourse has offered entertainment for nearly 200 years. During Gold Cup week, over 200,000 people come to watch the horse racing. Will it continue to draw in crowds?

The Royal Crescent, built between 1805 and 1825, is one of the grandest Regency buildings in Cheltenham. How will buildings change in future years?

...2001 GOLD CUP CANCELLED DUE TO FOOT-AND-MOUTH DISEASE...

The Brewery is a stylish eating and shopping centre but with more people shopping online, will places like this still exist in the future?

The GCHQ building is nicknamed 'the doughnut'. It is the largest single employer in Cheltenham. Will it still be around in 100 or 1,000 years' time?

The central courtyard area of the GCHQ building is so large that the Royal Albert Hall could fit inside it!

Will the Town Hall still be used in the future, or will it become a museum to show people how we lived?

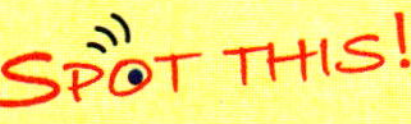

SPOT THIS!

The minotaur and hare statue can be seen in the Promenade. How tall are they compared to you?

How will they know?

Look around you. Which buildings do you think will be standing 200 years from now? What records do we keep that other people might one day read? Do DVDs and computers change what we can leave behind? What would you put in a time capsule?

Glossary

AD – a short way of writing the Latin words anno Domini, which mean 'in the year of our Lord', i.e. after the birth of Christ.

Ally (allies) – a person or country that supports another.

Artefact – another word for an object, often an archaeological one.

BC – a short way of writing 'before the birth of Christ'.

Besiege – when people try to capture a place by surrounding or blockading it.

Catholic – a member of the Christian religion that considers the pope to be the head of its church.

Cavalier – also known as a Royalist: someone who supported Charles I during the English Civil War.

Domesday Book – William the Conqueror sent his men all over England to check how much land and wealth was in the kingdom, and who owned it. The results of this survey were written in a book called the Domesday Book, which survives to this day.

Evacuees – children sent away from cities to the country during the war in order to avoid the bombing.

Grammar School – a secondary school that concentrates on academic subjects rather than practical ones.

Hypocaust – Roman central heating system.

Mosaic – a design made up of small pieces of glass or stone.

Parliamentarian – also known as a Roundhead: anyone who fought on the side of Parliament against Charles I in the English Civil War.

Priory – a religious house such as an abbey or monastery

Protestant – a member of the Christian religion that considers the king or queen to be the head of its church.

Ration Book – during World War Two, certain food was scarce and had to be rationed. Your Ration Book showed how much of this food you could have every week. Once you'd used it up, you wouldn't get any more until the next week.

Sedan Chair – a covered chair with poles, enabling it to be carried by one person at the back and one at the front.

Sentry – a soldier who guards the entrance to a place.

Smallpox – a disease that caused a fever and rash.

Spa – a mineral spring where the waters are believed to be good for the health.

Time Capsule – a container holding things from the present day which is buried in the ground for future generations to find.

Typhoid – a disease spread by contaminated food or water.

Vaccine – a type of medicine injected into people to prevent them getting a disease.

Workhouse – where poor people lived and worked when they had nowhere else to go.

Index

Acknowledgements

The author and publishers would like to thank the following people for their generous help:
Eric Miller and Sue Ryder Care

The publishers would like to thank the following people and organizations
for their permission to reproduce material on the following pages:

p5: NTPL – Ian Shaw; p7: Cheltenham Art Gallery & Museum, English Heritage Photo Library, shutterstock/
riekephotos; p9: Cheltenham Art Gallery & Museum; p11: The Rev Canon Andrew Dow, Rector & Area Dean
of Cheltenham; p13: Photographer Tracy Wilkinson – Archives Centre, King's College, Cambridge, GBR/22,
Photographer Tracy Wilkinson – Archives Centre, King's College, Cambridge, SJP/19, Sue Ryder Care, Leckhampton
Court; p14: Sudeley Castle; p15: Cheltenham Art Gallery & Museum; p16: Peter Barritt/Alamy; p17: Cheltenham
Art Gallery & Museum, Sudeley Castle; p19: Pictorial Press Ltd/Alamy; p22: Cheltenham Art Gallery & Museum;
p23: Cheltenham Art Gallery & Museum; p25: Holst Birthplace Museum; The National Archives, RG 11/2577;
p26: Cheltenham Art Gallery & Museum; p27: Cheltenham Art Gallery & Museum; p28: Crown Copyright,
reproduced with permission GCHQ

All other images copyright of Hometown World

Written by Lee Partridge
Educational consultant: Neil Thompson
Local history consultant: Ann-Rachel Harwood
Designed by Stephen Prosser

Illustrated by Kate Davies, Dynamo Ltd, Mike Hall, Tim Hutchinson, Peter Kent,
John MacGregor, Leighton Noyes, Tim Sutcliffe
Additional photographs by Alex Long

First published by HOMETOWN WORLD in 2010
Hometown World Ltd
7 Northumberland Buildings
Bath BA1 2JB

www.hometownworld.co.uk

Your **past**
Your **now**
Your **future**

Your **history4ever**

Mmm... Still love chocolate pudding!

My next one's going to have 2 wheels!

Trophy for the trendiest glasses?

I love you too!